FUNNY JOKES FOR 6 YEAR OLD KIDS

100+ Crazy Jokes That Will Make You Laugh Out Loud!

Cooper the Pooper

© **Copyright 2021 Cooper the Pooper - All rights reserved.**

The content contained within this book may not be reproduced, duplicated or transmitted without direct written permission from the author or the publisher.

Under no circumstances will any blame or legal responsibility be held against the publisher, or author, for any damages, reparation or monetary loss due to the information contained within this book, either directly or indirectly.

Legal Notice:
This book is copyright protected. It is only for personal use. You cannot amend, distribute, sell, use, quote or paraphrase any part, or the content within this book, without the consent of the author or publisher.

Disclaimer Notice:
Please note the information contained within this document is for educational and entertainment purposes only. All effort has been executed to present accurate, up to date, reliable, complete information. No warranties of any kind are declared or implied. Readers acknowledge that the author is not engaged in the rendering of legal, financial, medical or professional advice. The content within this book has been derived from various sources. Please consult a licensed professional before attempting any techniques outlined in this book.

By reading this document, the reader agrees that under no circumstances is the author responsible for any losses, direct or indirect, that are incurred as a result of the use of the information contained within this document, including, but not limited to, errors, omissions or inaccuracies.

TABLE OF CONTENTS

Table of Contents 3

Introduction 4

Chapter 1: Funny Jokes 6

Chapter 2: Crazy Jokes 18

Chapter 3: Laugh-out-Loud Jokes 30

Chapter 4: Knock-Knock Jokes 42

Chapter 5: Bonus Jokes 54

Final Words 66

INTRODUCTION

Top of the morning to you my fellow jokester – I hope you are ready to have some laughs.

Sorry, did I say some laughs? Well, I mean some a lot of laughs.

See, in your hand you hold one of my best pieces of work. You hold something that took me years to write. You have, in your hand, a book that is full to the brim with amazing jokes written just for six year old kids.

Trust me when I say this is not a book of normal jokes. In fact, I spent years travelling the world looking for the best jokes on the planet – and I am pretty sure I found all of them.

The jokes in this book cover every topic you think of. From cars to monsters to princesses, and then all the way back again, these jokes will have your sides splitting from laughing too hard.

And my favorite bit?

These jokes actually get funnier the more people you share them with.

Which means that as you read through this book you need to remember your favorites jokes so you can share them with your family, your closest friends, or even your entire class at school.

But make sure you take a minute or two between jokes – otherwise you might break a funny bone!

So, what in the world are you waiting for? Turn through these magical pages, dive on in, and start laughing at the funniest jokes for six year old kids on the planet.

What is a hot dog called on October 31st?

- A Hallo-weenie.

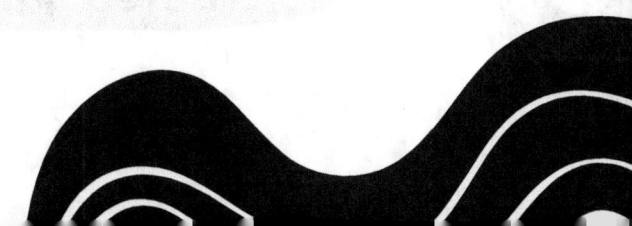

Do you know why Santa has 3 gardens?

- So he can ho-ho-ho.

3

What color is the wind?

- Blew.

4

What do kids play when they can't play with a phone?

- Bored games.

5

Why are teddy bears never hungry?
• They're always stuffed!

6

Why can't you ever tell a joke around glass?
• It could crack up.

How do you know when a bike is thinking?

- You can see its wheels turning.

What did the snowman ask the other snowman?

- Do you smell carrots?

9

What kind of music do balloons hate?

- Pop.

10

What do you call a sad strawberry?

- A blueberry.

What do you call a cow with no legs?

- **Ground beef!**

What's a skeleton's favorite instrument?

- **A trom-bone.**

13

Why can't Cinderella play soccer?

- Because she's always running away from the ball.

14

Why can't the music teacher start his car?

- His keys are on the piano.

I spent five minutes fixing a broken clock yesterday.

- At least, I think it was five minutes...

What did one hat say to the other?

- Stay here; I'm going on ahead.

What room doesn't have doors?

- A mushroom.

Why did the florist give so many kisses?

- She had two-lips.

19

What did the buffalo say when his son left?

- Bison!

20

Why are skeletons so evil?

- They are heartless!

Why should you never trust stairs?

- They're always up to something.

What is the most expensive kind of fish?

- A goldfish.

CHAPTER 2
CRAZY JOKES

1

What is brown and sticky?

- A stick!

2

What do you call a student who doesn't like math class?

- Calcu-hater.

Which hand is better to paint with?

- **Neither! A paint brush is better.**

Why are fish so smart?

- **Because they live in schools.**

5

What do you give a sick bird?

- **Tweetment!**

6

What is black and white and black and white and black and white and...?

- **A penguin falling down the stairs.**

Why does a flamingo lift up one leg?

- Because if it lifted both legs it would fall over!

What did one flea say to the other?

- Should we walk or take a dog?

9

What would you do if an elephant sat in front of you at a movie?

- **Miss most of the film.**

10

How do rabbits travel?

- **By hareplane.**

What time is it when an elephant sits on the fence?

- **Time to fix the fence!**

How do bees get to school?

- **By school buzz!**

13

What kind of keys do kids like to carry?

- Cookies!

14

What is a parent's favorite Christmas carol?

- Silent night.

Why did the student eat his homework?

- Because his teacher told him it was a piece of cake!

Why did the computer go to the doctor?

- Because it had a virus.

What are the strongest days of the week?

- **Saturday and Sunday. The rest are weak days.**

What do you do when you see an elephant with a basketball?

- **Get out of its way!**

19

What is a scarecrow's favorite fruit?

- **Straw-berries!**

20

What subject in school is easy for a witch?

- **Spell-ing!**

21

What do you get when you cross a computer with an elephant?

- **Lots of memory!**

22

What washes up on very small beaches?

- **Microwaves.**

CHAPTER 3
LAUGH-OUT-LOUD JOKES

1

Where did the school kittens go for their field trip?

- **To the mewseum.**

2

What's the difference between a TV and a newspaper?

- **Ever tried swatting a fly with a TV?**

Why can't your nose be 12 inches long?

- **Because then it would be a foot.**

What do you call a funny chicken?

- **A comedi-hen.**

5

How many letters are in the alphabet?

- There are 11 letters in "the alphabet."

6

What came after the dinosaur?

- Its tail!

7

How do you throw a party on Mars?

- **You planet.**

8

What's black and white and red all over?

- **An embarrassed zebra.**

9

What's a pirate's favorite subject in school?

- **Arrrrrrrrrrt.**

10

Why do seagulls like to live by the sea?

- **Because if they lived by the bay, they would be bagels!**

11

What do you do with a blue elephant?

• You try to cheer him up.

12

What side of the horse has the most hair?

• The outside.

13

What do you call a train that sneezes?

- Achoo-choo train.

14

What did one tomato say to the other tomato?

- You go ahead and I'll ketchup.

What is a bunny's motto?

- **Don't be mad; be hoppy!**

What did the spider do on the computer?

- **Made a website.**

What do ghosts eat?

- **Spook-hetti.**

Where do all the cool mice live?

- **In the mousepads.**

19

What do you call an elephant in a phone booth?

• Stuck.

20

Why do fish live in salt water?

• Because pepper makes them sneeze!

21

When do you go on red and stop on green?

- When you are eating a watermelon.

22

What do cats wear to bed?

- Paw-jamas.

Knock, knock!

Who's there?

D.

D who?

Depends. Do you want this pizza or not?

Knock, knock!

Who's there?

Noah.

Noah who?

Noah good pizza place around here?

3

Knock, knock!

Who's there?

Impatient cow.

Impatient cow who?

MOOOOOOO!

4

Knock, knock!

Who's there?

Eggs.

Eggs who?

Eggs-cuse me, you drove over my flowers.

Knock, knock!

Who's there?
Voodoo.

Voodoo who?
Voodoo you think you are?

Knock, knock!

Who's there?
Yourself.

Yourself who?
Your cell phone's ringing you better answer it.

7

Knock, knock!

Who's there?
Harold.

Harold who?
Harold do you think I am?

8

Knock, knock!

Who's there?
Alex.

Alex who?
Alex-plain when you open the door.

9

Knock, knock!

Who's there?

Anita.

Anita who?

Anita go to the bathroom.

10

Knock, knock!

Who's there?

Juliet.

Juliet who?

Juliet me in, please!

Knock, knock!

Who's there?
Ray.

Ray who?
Ray-ning cats and dogs out here. Please let me in!

Knock, knock!

Who's there?
Cows go.

Cows go who?
No, cows go MOO!

13

Knock, knock!

Who's there?

Watson.

Watson who?

What's on TV tonight?

14

Knock, knock!

Who's there?

Stu.

Stu who?

Stu late to ask questions.

Knock, knock!
Who's there?
Norton.
Norton who?
Norton nice to say!

Knock, knock!
Who's there?
Olivia.
Olivia who?
Olivia me alone.

Knock, knock!
Who's there?
Kenya.

Kenya who?
Kenya open the door, please?

Knock, knock!
Who's there?
Peas.

Peas who?
Peas let me in now!

Knock, knock!

Who's there?

Repeat.

Repeat who?

Who, who, who…

Knock, knock!

Who's there?

Snow.

Snow who?

Snowbody!

21

Knock, knock!

Who's there?

Waiter.

Waiter who?

Waiter I get my hands on you.

22

Knock, knock!

Who's there?

Justice.

Justice who?

Justice as I thought, you don't remember me!

1

Why are cats so good at video games?

- **Because they have nine lives.**

2

What state has a lot of dogs and cats?

- **Pets-sylvania.**

3

What goes up but never comes back down?

• Your age!

4

Where do you find keys that won't work in a lock?

• On a piano.

What has legs but can't walk?

- **A table.**

Which month has 28 days?

- **All of them, of course.**

How many tickles does it take to make an octopus laugh?

- Ten (tickles).

Why do dragons sleep during the day?

- So they can fight knights.

9

Where do people go when they have two broken legs?

- Nowhere!

10

Why did the burglar take a shower?

- He wanted to make a clean getaway.

11

Did you hear about the restaurant on the moon?

- The food is good, but there's no atmosphere.

12

Why did the scientist wear denim?

- Because he was a jean-ius.

13

Why do bees have sticky hair?

- **Because they use honeycombs.**

14

Did you hear about the two guys who stole a calendar?

- **They each got six months.**

15

What is it called when a cat wins a dog show?

- A cat-has-trophy.

16

How do you help an injured pig?

- Call a hambulance.

17

What did the llama say when he got kicked out of the zoo?

- "Alpaca my bags!"

18

How do bears keep cool?

- They use bear-conditioning.

19

Why do French people like to eat snails?

- **They can't stand fast food.**

20

What do you do if you see a spaceman?

- **Park your car, man.**

FINAL WORDS

Before you finish, I first wanted to thank you for reading my book.

I spent a very long time looking for the funniest I could find so I could write this book – and nothing makes me happier than knowing that great kids like you are reading them.

But please remember, you are not done yet.

Sure, you are at the end – but really, it is only the beginning.

Now you need to go back through this book and find all your favorite jokes. Then it is time to write them down on a special piece of paper, so you can share them with your friends and family.

After all, the only thing better than hearing a funny joke is telling a funny joke – so what are you waiting for?

Start sharing these amazing jokes with everyone you know and have a hilarious time while you do it!

www.ingramcontent.com/pod-product-compliance
Lightning Source LLC
Chambersburg PA
CBHW071408070526
44578CB00002B/518